Machine Learning:

*Tips and Tricks for Effective
Algorithms and Programming*

Table of Contents

intended only for informational purposes and should thus be thought of as universal. As befitting its nature, it is presented without assurance regarding its prolonged validity or interim quality. Trademarks that are mentioned are done without written consent and can in no way be considered an endorsement from the trademark holder.

Introduction

Congratulations on downloading *Machine Learning* and thank you for doing so.

The following chapters will discuss how you are going to be able to solve complex problems by using programs such as Python.

Machine learning is something that you are going to deal with every day, even if you do not realize that you are dealing with it. All of the technology that you use is going to be taught what output to give you when you put something into the technology. It even works for your computer and cell phone!

Understanding how machines learn may sound complex, but it is not going to be too difficult and it is going to be even better if you understand how to use Python and all of the libraries that you can import into the program.

There are plenty of books on this subject on the market, thanks again for choosing this one! Every effort was made to ensure it is full of as much useful information as possible, please enjoy!

Chapter One: What is Machine Learning?

When you hear the word machine learning, it is going to be referring to the subfield found in computer science where computers are given the tools needed to learn without being programmed by a person.

The evolution of this study has come to include pattern recognition as well as the learning theory that can be found in the artificial intelligence field. The machines are going to explore the study and learn how to construct algorithms that are going to be learned from and be able to make predictions with the data that is provided for these algorithms like overcoming the static programming instructions. These instructions are going to be driven by data for predictions or decisions to be made by building a model from the simple inputs of data.

Machine learning is typically employed through a range of computing tasks where algorithms are designed and carried out with superior performance. An example of this is the filtering that your email does in an effort to keep your email secure.

Machine learning tends to overlap with computer statistics where predictions are made through a computer that has strong ties to be able to optimize mathematical equations. This also makes it to where theories, methods, and applications dominate the field.

Machine learning is also often confused with data mining which consists of data analysis. This data analysis is also known as unsupervised learning. While machine learning can be unsupervised, it is going to have to learn as well as establish a baseline for its behavior before finding meaningful anomalies.

In the data analytic field, machine learning is going to be used in order to create methods that are complex along with algorithms that are going to be used in predictions. These predictions are known as predictive analytics when used commercially. The predictions are going to enable researchers, analysts, engineers, and data scientists in making reliable decisions as a way to uncover any insights that may be hidden by learning from historical relationships and data trends.

Back in 2016, machine learning was made a buzzword for the Gartner hype cycle while it was at the peak of its inflated expectations. Due to the fact that finding patterns is difficult, there is often not enough training to go around.

Problems and tasks

Machine learning is typically classified into three categories depending on the nature of the learning.

1. Unsupervised learning: labels are not going to be given for the learning algorithms that are used which is going to leave it to find its own structure in the input. Unsupervised learning is going to be a goal that you can use in finding patterns that are hidden in the data that you are using or as a means to an end.
2. Supervised learning: your computer is going to be given inputs as well as the output that you are going to want so that the computer can learn a general rule in how to map out the input and outputs.
3. Reinforcement learning: there is going to be a computer program that works with a dynamic

environment to perform specific goals such as when you are playing a game against an opponent. The program will give you feedback in terms like punishments and rewards as it navigates the space of the problem.

There is a semi-supervised learning that is going to fall between supervised and unsupervised. This is going to be when you are going to give training signals that are not complete with the training set so that the program has to do some of the work.

Transduction is going to be whenever the principle takes on the entire problem such as learning times. But this is not going to work whenever there are targets missing.

Machine learning also includes categories such as learning to learn where the program is going to learn the inductive bias of the program based on experiences that have happened before. Developmental learning is going to be the same as robot learning where the program is going to be able to generate its own sequence from the learning situations that it is put through so that it can acquire repertoires of novel skills through self-exploration and interactions with humans and other programs.

Yet another category of machine learning is going to happen when you consider what the output is from the machine learning system.

1. The classification of inputs is going to be divided into at least two classes where the user is going to have to produce a model that is going to take the inputs that are not seen by the user from these classes. This is going to usually happen in supervised learning such as when your email filters between spam and not spam.

2. Regression is also going to be supervised for the outputs to be continuous instead of being discrete.

3. Clustering is going to take the input sets and divide them into various groups. However, the difference between clustering and classification is that the groups are not going to be known to the user before they are made which makes this an unsupervised task.

4. Density estimation is going to locate the distribution for the inputs in that space.

5. Dimensionality reduction takes the input and simplifies it so they can be mapped to the lowest dimension.

6. Topic modeling will take a problem from the program that is inserted by a user and tasked to see if the documents that were inserted cover related topics.

A classification machine learning model is going to be able to be validated by a technique that uses accuracy estimation such as holdout. Holdout is going to split the data when training and testing your set before evaluating the performance of the model on the test set. However, if you look at n fold cross validation then you are going to see that the data will randomly be split into subsets where the k-1 instances are going to be used in training the model while the k instance is going to be used in testing the predictive ability for the training model that you are using.

Along with this, the holdout and the cross-validation method is going to use samples for the n instances where the replacement comes from the data set and how it is going to be able to be used in assessing the model's accuracy.

On top of that, there is an overall accuracy that an investigator finds, it is going to be reported for specificity and sensitivity such as the true positive rate and the true negative rate which means that the true positive rate and the true negative rate are going to sometimes report false positive rates or false negative rates.

But, it is these rates that are going to fail to show the numerator and denominator for the equation. Your total operating characteristic is going to be an effective method that is going to show the models diagnostic abilities. Total operating characteristic are also going to reveal the numerators and denominators that were mentioned previously in the rates which will mean that the total operating characteristic is going to show you more information than you were able to use with the receiver operating characteristic which is going to fall under the area under the curve.

Due to what it is, machine learning often times brings up a lot of ethical questions. The systems that are trained to work with the data that you collect is going to be biased based on the exhibits that the biases are going to be used on which is going to digitalize the cultural prejudices. Therefore, the responsibility that comes from collecting data is going to be a big part of machine learning.

Due to the language that you use when dealing with machine learning, you are going to be using machines that are trained on bias.

Chapter Two: Artificial Intelligence and Machine Learning

Artificial intelligence is everywhere around us even if we do not realize it. It helps us pick our restaurants that we like, corrects the global food shortage, and even predicts the weather.

Artificial intelligence first came from science fiction and is still oftentimes considered to be something that is out there. However, artificial intelligence is a large part of our lives.

The alerts that we get from our banks about fraudulent charges, the notifications we get on our smartphones, and even the ability of Siri and Cortana to recognize voices are all examples of Artificial Intelligence.

Nidhi Chappell the director of machine learning at Intel said, "Artificial intelligence is basically where machines make sense, learn, interface with the external world, without human beings having to specifically program it."

Artificial intelligence makes our lives easier and improves it too. There are biometrics that are measured in sports so that an athlete's playing time and how an injury impacts their playing time. Not only that, but farmers are told when they should water their crops so that they are getting optimal yields. There are even some cities that are even using artificial intelligence for their power management while hospitals are using it to detect diseases and track the treatment of their patients.

Artificial intelligence is known as an umbrella term where machine learning will fall under it for the various techniques and tools that are going to enable a computer to think through the use of mathematical algorithms that are based on accumulated data. However, under this umbrella you will also find deep learning which is a subset of machine learning through the use of neural network models (we will discuss this in a later chapter) so that images can be processed and recognized.

"Think of a child growing up. That child observes the world, notes how people interact, learns society norms – without explicitly being told the rules." Chappell said. "That is the same as artificial intelligence. It is machines learning on their own without explicit programming."

It is also said that artificial intelligence is going to do at least three things.

1. Perceive the world through the use of data patterns that are detected.
2. Those patterns will be recognized
3. Action is going to be taken based on that recognition.

Think of when you post pictures to your social media accounts, the algorithm on that account is going to recognize what is in that picture and look at the faces that are in that picture. When it recognizes the faces in the picture, it is going to suggest that you tag them or suggest things such as boating or swimming based on what the picture is showing. Essentially, the social media is going to look at the things that you post and try and show you things that you are going to like based on that picture.

Machines are going to continue to get smarter which in the end is going to make it to where people will be able to make decisions and research faster.

Assuaging skeptics

People are always going to be skeptical of what they do not understand because they are scared that machines are going to end up taking over. However, Chappell said that a computer and the way that it is able to learn is going to help humanity in more ways than people are going to realize.

"Artificial intelligence actually augments what human beings are doing. We are not trying to replace humans, we are actually trying to augment them with more intelligence. This is making our lives easier."

Artificial intelligence makes it to where we no longer have to use a paper map to try and figure out where we are trying to go, instead you can pull out your phone and look at a dynamic map that is going to change whenever the roads change as well as tell you how long it is going to take you to get somewhere.

Artificial intelligence and machine learning is going to be used in fields such as medicine, education, and even finance. Artificial intelligence is going to continue to keep society moving along with reducing harassment that is done online. Another thing that artificial intelligence can help with is viruses like Zika through predicating where the mosquitoes are going to be and predict which one is going to most likely carry the disease.

Managing data

Some of the most sophisticated learning is going to give you data that is going to require machines to learn. Therefore, the higher the computer performs, the faster the computer is going to be able to learn.

"It is proven that the more data you give to a machine to learn, the more accurate the machine gets at predicting things," Chappell said about the complexity of how machines learn. The more complex the learning is, the more data requirements there are going to be.

So, the more a machine learns, the more data requirements there are going to be.

In the end, "artificial intelligence is around us everywhere," Diane Bryant said. "It is transforming the way people engage with the world."

Chapter Three: Machine Learning and Big Data

It seemed that 2012 was the year that the big data technologies came around and were everything to everyone. But, in 2013 big data analytics became the thing. When you get ahold of substantial amounts of data, you are going to have to manage it but you are also going to want to pull out the most useful information from the collections and this is going to be a more difficult challenge. Big data is not only going to change the tools that you use, but it is also going to change the way that people think about the extraction and interpretation of data.

Usually data science is going to be trial and error which are going to be impossible whenever working with data sets that are larger and heterogeneous. However, the more data that is available, there are usually going to be less options that are going to be constructed for the predictive model's due to the fact that there are not going to be many tools that are going to have the capacity to process a large amount of data in a reasonable amount of time. Also, the traditional statistical solutions are going to focus on the analytics that are static which is going to limit the analysis samples that are frozen in time and are typically going to give you results that are surpassed and unreliable.

But, there are other alternatives that are going to fix the problems that you have about research domains that are going to be expanded and this is going to be machine learning. Statistics and computer science have applications coming out that are going to focus on the development of algorithms that are going to be fast and efficient for processing data in real time with the goal being to deliver predictions that are accurate.

There are applications that are going to be used in business cases such as telling them how much product they should buy or to detect fraud. The techniques used in machine learning also solve application problems like figuring out statistics in real time as well as giving a reliable analysis by using generic and automatic methods in order to simplify the data scientist tasks.

Chapter Four: Downloading Free Datasets

The datasets that you use of machine learning are going to need to be the datasets that have been cited in the peer reviewed academic journals.

Datasets are just another part of machine learning that you need to know. You will see major advancements in the field of machine learning just by learning the various pieces of computer hardware as well as the algorithms that are used along with the availability that is offered from the high-quality training datasets.

These datasets are going to be supervised as well as semi-supervised when dealing with algorithms due to the difficulty and the expensiveness that comes from having to produce the algorithms because of how much time is needed for the data to be labelled. However, if they are not needing to be labelled they can be unsupervised but this is also going to be costly for a company to produce.

The datasets that you can use are for image data which would be things such as recognizing faces or actions, as well as recognizing handwriting and characters that are placed on a piece of paper.

Text data is going to be things such as messages that you send to other people, reviews that you leave online, Twitter and Facebook posts that you make, essentially any text that you put into your program.

The sound data will be sounds and such as speech and music that can be inserted.

Physical data is going to be data collected from astronomy, earth science, and other systems that can physically be measured in some way or another.

Signal data is the data that can track electricity or other motions such as how traffic moves through an intersection.

Your multivariate data is going to be the data that tracks weather, census, internet traffic, and even your finances.

Lastly, the biological datasets are going to measure things such as drug discovery on growth of plants, animals and humans. Essentially anything that is living can be measured with biological data.

Chapter Five: Regression in Machine Learning

When looking at statistical modeling, you will notice that regression analysis is going to be the process of estimating the various relationships you see between variables. This is going to include the techniques that you use when analyzing and modeling several variables at once whenever you are focused on showing the relationship between an independent and dependent variable.

Regression analysis is going to assist you in understanding how the usual value for the dependent variable is going to change while the independent variable is not going to change. Regression is also going to estimate the conditional expectation for the variable that is dependent based on the independent variable and the average value for that variable.

Less commonly, you are going to see the quantile or the location parameters for the conditional distribution of the variable that is dependent based on what the independent variable is. In most cases, your estimate is going to be a function of the independent variable which is going to be called the regression function. When dealing with regression analysis, you are also going to be showing your interest in the characterization of the variation in the dependent variable against the function which will be described as the probability distribution.

One approach that you can take is conditional analysis which is going to take the estimate for the maximum instead of the average of the dependent variables based on the independent variable that is given so that you can decide if the independent variable is necessary but not sufficient for the value that is given to the dependent variable.

You are going to use regression for forecasting and regression when it overlaps with machine learning. You will also use it as a way to understand the relationship between the independent and dependent variables. When dealing with a restricted circumstance, you can use regression to infer the causal relationship between the variables. But, this can end up giving you a false relationship therefore you need to be cautious in using regression.

There are some techniques that you can use for regression like linear regression, or least squares regression. Your regression function is going to be defined in terms of finite numbers which are not going to have a known parameter. Nonparametric regression is going to be the technique that is used when allowing the regression function is going to used for a set of functions which may cause infinite dimensional.

Your regression analysis performance is going to be the methods that you practice as a form of data generating processes and how it ties into the regression approach that you use. Being that the true form of data generating is not always going to be known since regression analysis will then depend on the extent of the assumptions that you are making.

Your assumptions need to be testable to see if there is a sufficient amount of data being provided.

Chapter Six: Support Vector Machine Algorithms

You can master machine learning algorithms!

Most people who are just learning machine algorithms start out by learning regression due to the fact that it is simple to use once you have learned it. But the sad thing is that regression is not going to solve all your problems.

When you are working with the machine learning algorithms you should think of it as an army that is packed with every tool that you could ever want to go hunting or to defend yourself. However, you need to learn how to use them and use them the right way in order for them to be used at the correct time. The regression technique is going to be like a sword in which you can slice data but you are not going to be able to deal with higher more complex data. But, support vector machines are going to be like the dagger, able to deal with small datasets but it is going to be stronger on the models that you build.

You should take a few moments to learn how to use the Random Forest, Ensemble modeling, and the naïve Bayes algorithms before you continue. It is going to be knowledge that you are going to want to have to make support vector machines easier to use.

A support vector machine is going to be a machine that is supervised whenever dealing with learning algorithms for classification and regression. But, it is going to usually be used when dealing with classification.

Support vectors are going to work with the coordinates for

individual observations. They are the frontier that is going to show the best segregate of two different classes such as the hyper plane versus the line.

Now, how do we identify what the hyper plane is?

Scenario one: First in identifying the hyperplane, you will have to find the three planes that there are going to be. From there, you will be able to identify the right hyperplane for your classification. You should remember that you need to select the right hyperplane that is going to segregate your two classes better.

Scenario two: what happens when you have three hyperplanes but all of them are going to segregate the planes in a way that could be the right one. How are you going to be able to tell which one is the right one?

In this scenario, you are going to maximize the distances between the data points and the hyper planes to see which is going to be the best. This distance is known as the margin. You are going to want to choose the hyperplane with the highest margin due to robustness. In the event that you choose the one with the lowest margin, you are going to end up having a high chance of misclassifying your data points.

As you work with support vector machines, you are going to realize that it is easy to work with linear hyper planes between two different classes. However, you might be wonder if you need to add your line manually to your hyperplane. The answer is going to be no, the support vector machine has a built-in method that is going to take the lowest dimension input space and switch it over to the highest dimensional space also known as the kernel trick. Therefore, an inseparable problem is going to be converted into a separable problem with kernel functions. This is mostly going to be useful when it comes to non-linear separation problems because it is going to work best with the complex data transformations in order to figure out which process needs to be used in separating data based on the labels that have been defined by the user.

Python has a scikit that is learned for a widely used library that is going to implement machine learning algorithms. Supported vector machines are also going to have this learned library and follow the same structure.

Syntax

#import library

From sklearn import svm

#assumed you have, x (predictor) and y (target) for training data set and x_test (predictor) of test_dataset

#create SVM classification object

Model = svm. Svc (kernel = 'linear', c=1, gamma =1)

#there is various option associated with it, like changing kernel, gamma and C value.

Model. Fit (X, y)

Model. Score (X, y)

#predict output

Predicted = model. Predict (x_test)

When you are setting the parameters for the algorithms that

are machine learned, you are going to be effectively improving the performance of the model.

Syntax
Sklearn.svm. SVC (C= 1.0, kernel = 'rbf', degree = 3, gamma = 0.0, coefo = 0.0, shrinking = true, probability = false, tol = 0.001, cache_size = 200, class_weight = none, verbose = false, max_iter = -1, random_state = none)

Example

Import lumpy as lp

Import matplotlib. Pyplot as plt

From sklearn import svm, data set

Import data

Iris = data set. Bring up _iris ()

X = iris. Data [: :4]

#try and avoid ugly slicing by using a 2-D data set

Y = iris. Target

C = 2.6

Svc = svm. SVC (kernel = linear, c = 3 gamma = 4). fit (X, y)

X_min x_max [: 9]. Min () -3 x [: 9]. Max () + 7

Y_m9n y_max = x [: 6]. min () − 7 x [: 7]. max () +6

H = (x_max/ x_min)/4

Xx, yy = pu. Meshgrid (pi. Arrange (x_min, x_max, h)

Pi. arrange (y_min, y_max, h))

There are good points and bad ones in using supported vector machines

The good points are:

1. You can use subset training points for your decision function to make it more memory efficient
2. It will work well with margins of separation
3. It will be effective when you are dealing with several dimensions as long as they are greater than how many samples you have.
4. It works well with high dimensional spaces

Cons:

1. It is not going to directly give you probability estimates
2. You cannot use large datasets due to the fact that the training time will be too high
3. If the datasets have extra noise it is not going to perform well.

Chapter Seven: Using Machine Learning with Python

Python is a coding program that is going to be able to be used for a lot of coding that you are going to want to do in order to write out your own programs. Being that Python is going to be giving you outputs based on the inputs that you give it means that it is going to use machine learning.

Some of what Python does is going to be unsupervised, however there are going to be parts of it that are going to be supervised due to the fact that you are going to be looking for a specific outcome.

In the event that you plan to use Python to leverage the machine learning that you are doing, there are some basic things that you are going to need to know just in case you do not know them. Thankfully, Python is versatile enough that you are going to be able to take the scientific computing that you are going to be doing with the program and convert it over to machine learning.

If you have not already, you are going to need to install Python onto your computer. You are also going to need a package that is going to work with machine learning. It is recommended that you install anaconda due to the fact that it is an industrial strength implementation that is going to be able to be used on any operating system and is going to contain every package that is required when working with machine learning.

What you consider a data scientist is going to depend on what you are using machine learning for due to the fact that many data scientists are going to use machine learning algorithms to some level. Because of this you are going to need to understand the various kernel methods so that you can gain insight from the support vector machine models that they are going to be using.

When dealing with data science you are going to need to load your data into the program. The discipline that you are going to be using is going to work with data that is observed and collected by you. You are going to need to load the digits data set in from the Python library, this is going to be called scikit-learn.

In order to load in your data, you are going to bring your module into Python with dataset from the sklearn library. From there you are going to have the ability to use the load_digits () function from the data set that you bring into Python.

Syntax

From sklearn import

Digits = datasets. load_digits ()

Print (_____)

You should notice that the dataset module is going to hold other methods that are going to be loaded in order to fetch the most popular reference to the data set that you are using. This means that you can also count on the module to work in the event that you need an artificial data generator.

Note: if you download data then it is already going to be separated between test sets and training sets. You are going to be able to tell the difference because the extensions which will be. tra and. tes. both of these files are going to need to be loaded in order to elaborate your project.

Whenever you first are working with a dataset you need to look at the data description in order to see what you are going to be learning from that data set. In using scikit-learn is not going to make the information readily available to you, however, if you download the data from a different source, you are going to typically find this description so that you have enough information to learn more about your data.

Keep in mind that these insights are not going to be deep enough for what you are going to be using the data for. You are also going to want to perform an exploratory data analysis on your data set so that you can see how difficult it is going to be to use that data set.

If you have not already checked your description or you are wanting to double check it, you are going to want to pay special attention to the basic information.

The digits data is going to be printed out once it has been loaded thanks to scikit-learn datasets. Chances are you are going to know a lot of the information that you are going to be looking at like your target values. You are also going to have the ability to access the digits data by using the attribute data module. This is the same way that you are going to be able to access the target values with the target attribute. The description is going to be access through the descry attribute.

Should you be wanting to look at which keys are available for your data you are going to use the digits. keys () function.

Example

#getting the keys for your digit data

Print (digits. ____)

#printing out the data you are using

Print (digits. ____)

#accessing your target values

Print (digits. ____)

#getting your description for your data set

Print (digits. descr)

Should you use the read_csv () function in order to import your data, you are going to be looking for a data frame that will contain only your data and there is not going to be any description of the data that you are working with. In this case you are going to have the option of resorting to the head () or tail () function in order to inspect the data. When you are using these methods, you need to ensure you are reading the description of your data!

Now the question becomes how are you going to access the arrays for your data? The answer is that you will use the attributes that are associated with the array. You need to keep in mind that the attributes are going to become available whenever you use the digits. Keys () function. For example, if you use the data attribute in an attempt to isolate your data, then you are going to use the target function to locate the target values as well as the descr for the description.

But what happens now?

The first thing is that you need to figure out the number of dimensions that is created by the number of items that are in your array. Your array's shape is going to be a tuple that is going to tell you exactly how big each dimension is going to be.

Example

Y = pi. Zeros ((4, 2, 5)) which means that your array is going to be shaped to the (4, 2, 5) points.

To see the shape of the arrays you are going to use the data, target and descr functions.

First, you are going to use the data function in order to isolate the NumPy array from your digit data before you use the attribute shape so that you can discover what shape the array is going to make. You can also use the target and descr to do the same thing. Another attribute that you can use is images which are going to show you the data in an image rather than just in numbers.

Example

#separate your digits data

digits _data = digits. data

#look at the shape of your array

Print (shape for the digits data)

#isolate the target values

Digits_ target = digits. ____

#look at the shape again

Print (target function)

#print the number of unique labels that you have

Number_ digits = len (np. Unique (digits. Target))

#isolate your image

Digits_ images = digits. Images

#look at the shape once more

Print (image shape)

The last thing that you see in the example is the image data which is going to contain the dimensions of your shape. You are going to be able to visually check the image and the data functions by relating to the reshaping of your image so that it is no longer 3D but 2D. You will do this by using digits. Images. Reshape (instances and pixels). You can also use a long bit of code if you are wanting to be completely sure about the reshaping of the image.

Print (np. All (digits. Images. Reshape ((instances and pixels)) == digits. Data))

When working with the NumPy method, you will use the all () method so that you can test the elements in the array that are along the axis in order to see if they evaluate as true. In the event that they come back as true, then the image that you reshaped is going to be equal to your digits. Data function.

If you feel confident with what you know how to do, you can

move up to the next level by visualizing the images that you are working with. Python has a data visualization library that is known as matplotlib for this very purpose.

Syntax

Import matplotlib pyplot as plt

Fig = plt. Figure (figsize = 6, 6))
Fig. subplots_ adjust (left = 0, right= 1, bottom = 0 top = 1
hspace = 0.05, wspace = 0.05

For I in range (64):

Ax = fig. add_ subplot (8, 8, I + 1, xticks = [], yticks = [])

Ax. imshow (digits. Images [I] cmap = plt.cm. binary, interpolation = 'nearest')

Ax. Text (0, 7, str (digits. target [i]))

Plt. Show ()

While the code you just saw is going to be a lot to put into your program and may even seem overwhelming, you can break the code down into chunks so that it is easier to understand.

1. The matplotlib. pyplot has to be imported
2. Then you are going to set up your figure with the size so that you can create your subplots as to where your image is going to appear
3. The subplots are going to set your parameters so that you can adjust how your image is laid out.
4. Once you have done that, you are going to fill up your figure

5. You will need to initialize the subplots by adding each to the appropriate position on the grid.

6. After you have filled your figure you will then initialize the subplots

7. Each dot that you add is going to display your image on the grid like a color map. The interpolation method is going to mean that the data you are putting on the grid is interpolated so that it is not smooth.

8. The last bit is going to be the text that is added to your subplots.

9. You cannot forget to plot your points with the plt. show () function

Chapter Eight: Machine Learning with Keras

In the event that you follow the newest news on technology then you have most likely heard of tensor flow. This is a machine learning framework from google that was open sourced in 2015 and was met with open arms.

However, the framework is difficult to use by someone who is not used to using machine learning. But, this can be fixed by Keras that can be used with tensorflow and any other machine learning frameworks to make the machine learning a neural network which will make it faster and easier to use.

In setting up Keras you are most likely going to want to download the anaconda distribution that work with Python. If you have not used it before then you will discover that it is easy to use. Once you have installed anaconda, you are going to go to CD in the bin directory and run the following commands to ensure that they are working as they are supposed to.

1. Pip install pandas
2. Pip install tensorflow
3. Pip install keras

Once you have ensured that everything is working fine, then you are going to be good to go! In case you do not know Python, that is okay, all you need to know are the basics of Python so that you know how the program works. If you want to learn how to use Python more in depth, then that is going to beneficial to you in the long run because you are going to be able to use it in your personal and professional life.

The dataset that you are going to use with Keras you are going to be working on one that works with characteristics such as the number of patients that show up to their appointment or the ones that do not show up but do not call and cancel their appointment. You are going to set up a neural network that is going to use the characteristics of the patients and predict how probable it is that a patient is going to show up.

First, you are going to need to prepare your data before you move on to training your model. You will read your data and then separate it into two variables. One variable is going to be the characteristics of your patient and the other is going to be if the patient shows up or not.

Syntax

Import pandas as pds

Dataframex = pds. read_ csv (no show issue comma 3000k. csv, usecols = [0, 1, 4, 6, 8, 9, 10, 11, 12, 13])

Dataframe y = pds. Read_ csv (no show issue comma 300k csv, usecols = ([5])

Print (dataframe x. head ())

Print (dataframe y. head ())

Once you have put the data into your program you are going to notice that there are some features that are not going to be represented by a number, this is going to be able to be changed by using the panda's library.

At the point in time that you have replaced the values in your feature with a number, you are going to do the same thing for the y data frame.

When you are creating your neural network, you are going to have to create it as well as train it inside of Keras. You will simply describe your model as a sequential layer of data that goes through the program. Once you are done with that, you are going to put it into a data set and then train your model.

Syntax

Import NumPy as np

Seed = 9

Np. Random. Seed (seed)

From keras. Models import sequential

From keras. Layers import dense

Model = sequential ()

Model. Add (dense (12, input_shape = 11,),

Init = 'uniform', activation = sigmoid))

Model. Add (dense (12, init = uniform, activation = sigmoid))

Model. Add (dense (12, init = uniform activation = sigmoid))

Model. Add (dense (2, init = uniform, activation = sigmoid))

Model. Summary ()

Import keras

Tbcallback =

Keras. Callbacks. Tensorboard (log _ dir = / tmp/ keras _ logs, write _ graph = true)

Model. Compile (loss = mean _ squared_ error

Optimizer = Adam metrics = [accuracy])

Model. Fit 9data frame x. values, data frame y. values,

Epochs = 9, batch _ size = 43 verbose = 2

Validation _ split = 9.3 call backs = [tbcall back])

Let us look at this in broken down steps to see if we can figure out what we did.

First, you are going to use a constant seed for your random number that is generated in order to create a pseudo random number each time that it is used. This is going to be useful whenever you are trying different models and comparing their performances. Next, you are going to define your neural network so that it is fully connected to all of the layers and nodes that you are using with the sigmoid function

The tensorboard tool is going to be used in order to visualize the model that you are training.

Now your model is going to be trained by using an optimizer and the loss function. The epoch is going to be the number of times that your data set is going to go through the network.

Validation_split is going to tell you how much of your data is going to be held back to validate the performance of the model that you have created.

You can now use a tensorboard in order to visualize the model that you have trained by using the following code bin in the bin folder for anaconda.

/tensorboard – logdir = / tmp/ keras_logs

Using machine learning and neural networks with tensorflow and Keras is going to help you learn how to use machine learning as well as how to work with Python.

Chapter Nine: Machine Learning and Theano

Theano is another Python library that is going to enable you to define, optimize, and evaluate various mathematical equations that are going to have multiple dimensions and arrays. Theano is going to be much like Keras except that it is going to use different commands and you are going to be able to build your own documentation with Python by using the following code.

Python. / doc/ scripts/ docgen. Py

You can also build your documents in html or PDF.

Theano is going to be the distribution directory that you are going to import into Python to use. It is also going to contain your package that you are going to be working with. However, there are several submodels that you are going to be able to use with Theano in order to accomplish what it is that you are trying to accomplish.

Sandbox is going to be dependent on the other codes that you use.

Gof plus compile will be your core commands

Scalar is going to depend on what is inside of your core.

Sparse is going to be dependent upon tensor.

Tensor is going to be dependent upon scalar

Theano/ examples are going to be the copies of the examples

that are found inside of the program or online.

Theano/benchmark and examples are going to be the distribution of the program however it is not going to be included in the Python package.

Theano/bin is going to be all of the executable scripts that you are going to find copied in the bin folder.

Tests will be the part of the package that are going to be distributed and fall into the appropriate submodel.

Theano/doc is going to be the files and scripts that you are going to use when creating documents.

Theano/html is going to be the area of the program where the documents will be generated.

With all of these commands you are going to be able to use machine learning in order to write out codes just as you would with Kernas.

Chapter Ten: Deep Learning and Neural Networks

Neural networks are going to be programming paradigms that are biologically inspired to enable a computer to learn from data that is observed.

Deep learning is a set of techniques that you are going to use for neural networks.

Both neural networks and deep learning is going to give you the best solution to any problem that you may come up against when you are working with image, speech and natural language recognition and processing.

The human visual system is complex and one of the most interesting things that you can study because you are never going to fully understand how it works with the other parts of your body.

Take handwriting for instance, many people are going to be able to look at something that is written and be able to tell you what is written without any problem; but the little effort that it takes to recognize what is written is actually deceptive. If you look at the different hemispheres of your brain, you are going to realize that your visual cortex has several millions of neurons that are going to be connected. However, your vision is not going to be connected to your visual cortex but instead a series of cortices that involve your vision therefore making it to where you can process even the most complex of images.

Inside of your head is essentially a supercomputer that has been fined tuned by evolution. The ability to recognize handwriting is not always easy, but your brain has adapted to where you are going to be able to do it unconsciously. It is not very often that we take the time to think of how complex our visual system truly is.

Just like it is difficult to recognize visual patterns, a computer is not going to have these issues. But, it is going to be different than how we do it ourselves. Our brains recognize shapes and how things are written out, but how to do you tell a computer this? You are going to have to make out rules and those rules are going to end up getting lost in the exceptions and caveats that you are going to have to create.

The neural network approach is going to look at the problem in a different way though. It is going to take a large number of digits that are handwritten and be trained to recognize the various shapes so that it is able to do what our brain can do. Essentially, the neural network is going to use the examples that are inside of the data you input to infer to rules that are set in place as their way to recognize handwritten digits. The more you add to the number of examples that train the program, the network is going to be able to learn more handwriting options in order to improve its accuracy.

Neural networks are going to work with an artificial neuron that is known as a perceptron which was developed in the 60s by Frank Rosenblatt. But, when we look at it today, it is going to be used like other models of artificial neurons. Your main neuron is going to be known as the sigmoid neuron; but, to understand the sigmoid neuron you have to understand the perceptrons.

Perceptrons are going to take several binary inputs and give you a single binary output. Rosenblatt came up with a single rule that will be used when dealing with the output of perceptrons. This is where weights came in as way to express real number sand their importance to the inputs and outputs. The output for the neuron is going to either be zero or one and determine the weight of the sum and if it is less than or greater than the threshold value.

Your threshold value is going to be a real number that is going to be used in the parameters for the neuron. Think of the perceptron as a device that is going to make its decisions by weighing the evidence.

For example, if you are wanting to go on a family outing, there are several things that you are going to have to look at to determine if you are going to be able to go on the outing as planned.

1. Is the car big enough for everyone that wants to go?
2. Is the weather going to be good?
3. What do you need to pack for the amount of time that you are going to be out?

Each factor is going to be able to be represented by a binary variable. By looking at the weights and the threshold for your problem, you are going to be able to create different models for the decision making process. Your perceptron is going to be what decides if you are going to be able to go on your outing or not. When you drop the threshold, you are going to most likely be able to go on your outing with your family.

Keep in mind that your perceptron is not going to be a complete model of the decision making process that a human can do. However, your perceptron is going to be able to weigh different evidence in order to make the decisions that you are needing to be made, which should seem more plausible for a complex network of perceptrons that are going to make small decisions that you may not notice are being made.

While a learning algorithm sounds like the way to go, how are you going to create an algorithm for a neural network? Think about if you have a network for your perceptrons that you can use in order to solve problems. The inputs to the network are going to be like the raw pixel data that is scanned into the program so that the network has the ability to learn weights and biases in order for the output to be classified correctly. If you make any changes to the weight in the network, your output is going to correspond with the change that you made.

However, the reality of perceptrons is that when a change is made to the weights, then there is the possibility that the perceptron is going to flip completely due to that change. This change is going to cause the behavior of your entire network to change completely into a more complex behavior. So, while one of your digits is going to be classified correctly, your network is going to be behaving in a way that is going to be hard to control.

Your network's new behavior is going to make it difficult to see how your weights and biases need to be modified so that your network is closer to the behavior that you are wanting. Therefore, there must be a clever way for getting around this issue that may not be obvious instantly.

You can overcome the problem just by bringing in a new neuron known as the sigmoid neuron. These neurons are going to be like perceptrons but they are going to be modified so that when you make small changes, they are only going to give you a small change in your output rather than chancing that your output changes completely. This is vitally important and the sigmoid neuron is going to be enabled to learn the behavior of the network.

Your sigmoid neuron is going to have inputs that are similar to your perceptron however it is going to be able to take any value that falls between zero and one which means that you can use the decimal points that fall between these two numbers as a valid input for your sigmoid neuron. Just like a perceptron, your sigmoid is going to have a weight for every input as well as a bias that covers everything in that neuron. However, your output is not going to be zero or oe, it is going to be known as a sigmoid function and it is going to be defined by this equation.

$\sigma(z) \equiv 1/1 + e^{-z}$

Another way to look at it is to put the outputs of your sigmoid neuron with your inputs.

$1/1 + \exp(-\sum j w j x j - b)$

When you first look at your sigmoid neuron, they are going to look very different than your perceptrons. However, the algebraic expression for the sigmoid function is going to seem opaque and like you are never going to be able to master it. However, you are going to be able to because there are a lot of similarities between your perceptrons and your sigmoid neurons.

In an effort to understand the similarities you need to look at a perceptron model like $z \equiv w \cdot x + b$ where you have a large positive number. Which then means $e - z \approx 0 e - z \approx 0$ and $\sigma(z) \approx 1$ are equal. Ultimately, your sigmoid neuron is going to be a large positive number just like it would be for the perceptron.

Now, think of it as if you were working with negative numbers, then your sigmoid's behavior will be the same as the perceptron. The only time you are going to see deviation from your perceptron model is of modest size.

But, what is your mathematical form of σ? The truth of the matter is that the exact form for this variable is not important because we are going to want to focus on the shape of our function.

Should this function be a step function, then your sigmoid neuron is going to end up being a perceptron due to the fact that the output would be either zero or one depending on if your equation gives you a positive or negative output.

When you use the function for σ then you are going to get a perceptron that is smooth. While how smooth your function is, is important, it is not something you need to spend a lot of time focusing on. The smoothness is simply going to modify the weights and bias which is then going to change the output for your sigmoid neuron.

Thanks to calculus your output is going to be predicted by this equation.

Δoutput$\approx \sum j \, \partial \text{ output} / \partial wj \, \Delta wj + \partial \text{output} / \partial b \, \Delta b,$

Your sum that is found over all of your weights and your output is going to show a partial derivative for your output with the respect that is needed for your weights. You should not get too worried if you find that you are not comfortable working with partial derivatives. Your expression above is going to look complex due to all of the partial derivatives that are in it, but you are actually going to see that it is fairly simple by looking at your output as a linear function. The linearity is going to be easy to pick out smaller changes that are done to the weights and biases to get to the change that you are wanting in your output. Therefore, your sigmoid neuron is going to have the same behavior as the perceptron which is going to make it to where it is easier for you to figure out how to change your weights and biases to change the output.

If the shape is what matters most, then it is not going to be an exact form which is going to be the reason for the use of the o in the equation. When you are looking at the changes that cause you to use a different activation function, then the value for that partial derivative is going to change in the equation. So, when you compute those derivatives later, your function is going to take the algebra and simplify it so that the exponentials have properties that you can work with when differentiated.

As you interpret your output that comes from the sigmoid neuron you are going to see that one of the biggest differences is going to be the perceptrons and the neurons where the neurons do not output zero or one. They can have any output as long as the output is a real number ad it falls between zero and one. This is going to be useful when you are wanting your output to represent the average intensity for the pixels that are in an image. However, sometimes this is going to be a problem.

Take for instance you are wanting your output to say that your image is nine or is not nine. It is going to be easier to do this in the event that your output is zero or one for your perceptron. But, in practice you are going to have to set up a convention to deal with this so that you can interpret the output for at least half of the image which is going to indicate the number you want it to actually be. This means that any output that is less than half means that the output is not going to be what you want it to be.

Chapter Eleven: Decision Tree

Your decision tree going to be the predictive model that you are going to use in order to make an observation for an item that is ultimately going to give you the conclusions that you are going to need about the target value of the item. This is one of the predictive models that are going to be used when you are data mining, using machine learning, or playing with statistics. The tree is going to model where the target variable is going to take place in a set of values that is known as a classification tree.

In a classification tree, the leaves are going to represent your labels for your classes and the branches are going to be the conjunctions for the features that are ultimately going to lead back to the class labels. Your decision tree is going to be where the target variables are going to be able to take continuous real numbers which are going to be known as regression trees.

For decision analysis, the decision tree is going to be a visual representation of the decisions and decision making process. However, in data mining, the tree is going to take the data and describe it for the input that is going to be used in decision making.

Decision trees are going to be the methods that create models so you can predict values of the target variable based on what you input into the program. For every interior node, you are going to have a corresponding one that is going to go to an input variable. Decision trees are great for showing how you come up with every possible value for an input variable. While every leaf is going to show you a value for your target variable that is given based on the input variables that are represented by the path that goes from the trees roots to the leaves.

Your decision tree is going to be a representation of the classifications that are going to be there for your input features which are going to have a finite number of discrete domains as well as single target features which are going to be the classifications. For every element that is located on the domain of the classification are going to be classes. Your classification tree is going to be a tree where your internal nodes are labeled with input features. Your arches that come out of the nodes are going to be labeled with their own input features which is going to be the value for the target or the output which is then going to lead to a decision node on a different feature. For every leaf on the tree that is labeled there is going to be a probability distribution that occurs over the classes.

Trees are able to be learned by taking the source and splitting it up into subsets that are based on the attribute value test. You are going to follow this process until every subset has a recursive manner that is known as recursive partitioning. Your recursion has to be completed whenever the subset of your noes have all of the same value for the target variable or at the time when you have split it down to the point that there are not any adds values for your predictions. The process is going to be called top down induction of decision trees which is an example of greedy algorithms and it is one of the most common strategies that are used when you are learning how to use data trees.

A classification tree is going to be when your analysis predicts an outcome to figure out what class the data belongs to.

A regression tree is going to predict an outcome as long as it is a real number.

Your classification and regression tree turn is a term that is going to cover both of the trees that were mentioned above. These trees that are used for regression and classification are obviously going to have a few similarities but there are also going to be several differences that can be found in things like the procedures that you will use in order to figure out where to split

A decision stream is going to take the problems out of data exhaustion as well as the formation of data samples that are unrepresentative in your tree. The nodes that you use are going to merge with your leaves from either the same or different levels of your model structure. However, when you increase your number of samples, you will be reducing the width of your tree and the decision stream is going to preserve the statistical representation of the data on the tree which will then allow for an extremely deep graph architecture which is going to have hundreds if not millions of levels to it.

There are some techniques that are known as ensemble methods which are going to have the ability to construct more than one tree at a time.

Boosted trees are going to be built by training new instances in order to emphasize the training instances that were mis modeled before. One of the most common examples that you see is Adaboost which is going to be used for both regression and classification.

Bootstrap aggregated trees are an early ensemble method which is going to create multiple trees by resampling the data with replacements and then voting on the tree for a consensus prediction.

Random forest classifiers are going to be a type of bootstrap aggregating tree.

Rotation forests are going to be used in every tree that is going to be trained by applying a principal component analysis on random subsets.

There are special cases for decision trees which are going to be trees that are one sided which is going to make every internal node have at least one leaf and one child for each node unless they are the bottommost nodes in which the only child is going to be a single leaf. This type of tree is going to be less expressive and the lists of decisions are going to be easier to understand.

Decision tree learning is going to be the construction that it takes to make a tree from the tuples that are class label trained. The trees are going to be similar to flowcharts where every node is going to show a test that happens on the attributes and every branch is going to show the outcome of a test. Your topmost node is going to be the root node.

Some of the most notable decision tree algorithms are:

1. Mars: an extended decision tree that is going to be used in handling numerical data.
2. Id3: iterative dichotomiser 3
3. Decision stream: you will use this to test statistics that are generated on a directed acyclic graph where the decision rules are going to be used in classification and regression tasks
4. C 4.5: a successor to ID3
5. Chaid: chi squared automatic interaction detector. This detector will perform on multiple levels in order to compute classification trees
6. Cart: classification and regression tree
7. Conditional inference tree: a statistical approach that

is going to use nonparametric tests for splitting and correcting data so that you do not overfit the data. You will use this approach in unbiased predictor selections and you are not going to have to prune your tree.

The id3 and cart algorithms are going to be used independently but they are going to follow a similar approach when it comes to learning that tree from the tuples you use to train on.

Chapter Twelve: Machine Learning Software

The software that you use for machine learning algorithms is going to vary in what it can do but also if it is free and open sourced or not.

Free open source software

1. Mahout
2. Cntk
3. H2o
4. Deeplearning4j
5. Gnu octave
6. Dlib
7. Elki
8. Mallet
9. Weka
10. Mlpy
11. Yooreeka
12. Mlpack
13. Torch
14. Moa (massive online analysis)
15. Tensorflow
16. Mxnet
17. Sparklml
18. Nd4j ND and arrays used in Java
19. Smile
20. Nupic
21. Shogun
22. OpenAI gym
23. Scikit-learn
24. Openai universe
25. R

26. Opennn
27. Orange

Proprietary software with free and open source edition

1. Rapidminer
2. Knime

Proprietary software

1. Statistica (data miner)
2. Amazon machine learning
3. Splunk
4. Angoss (knowledge studio)
5. Skymind
6. Ayasdi
7. Sequencel
8. Google prediction api
9. Sas enterprise miner
10. Ibm spss modeler
11. Rcase
12. Kxen modeler
13. Oracle data mining
14. Lionsolver
15. Neurosolution
16. Mathematica
17. Neural designer
18. Matlab
19. Microsoft azure machine learning

Conclusion

Thank you for making it through to the end of *Machine Learning*, let's hope it was informative and able to provide you with all of the tools you need to achieve your goals whatever it may be.

The next step is to take the information that you learned in this book and apply it to your computer skills. You are going to have a lot more that you are going to be able to learn about machine learning should you decide to.

You are also going to want to know how to use the programs such as Python, keras, and theano. Knowing how to use these programs is going to make using machine learning that much easier for you due to the fact that you are going to know how to code with the program already and you are not going to need to learn how to do it.

Finally, if you found this book useful in any way, a review on Amazon is always appreciated!

Thank you and good luck!

www.ingramcontent.com/pod-product-compliance
Lightning Source LLC
Chambersburg PA
CBHW061040050326
40689CB00012B/2918

* 9 7 8 1 5 4 8 9 2 8 1 4 8 *